# BECOME A FAN ON FACEBOOK
# AND SHARE THE EXPERIENCE WITH OTHERS!

## "Clemy's Pancake House" - A Revisionist Public Domain Parody

2007-2010 © Kevin Michael Mooney and Ken Kula.

All Rights Reserved.

ISBN: 978-0-615-34422-5

ISBN: 0615344224

New-Wolf Moon Publishing

This book, or portions thereof, may not be reprinted without the expressed written permission of Kevin M. Mooney and Ken Kula. For reprint permission, please contact clemys@sbcglobal.net.

*To my children who dreamed of a better life for Clemy
and for my wife who makes this life better.*

**-Kevin**


*To my wife and our three children
whose love of reading make this all worthwhile.*

**-Ken**

Back in 1849, a man named Mr. Tine lived
in Chicago, Illinois with his daughter, Clemy.


One morning while reading the paper and eating Clemy's fine pancakes,
Mr. Tine read that miners in California had found some gold.
"By Gosh, Clemy, I think we aught a git some a that gold!
Pack up your belongins and hitch up those mules.
We're heading for California!" And they were off.

# C

They settled in a cavern in a canyon and began mining for gold.

One morning, while feeding the ducks along the river's edge,

Clemy tripped and fell into the water with a big splash!

Mr. Tine, he was no swimmer, and could not help his girl.

She floated out of sight, under the water,

lost to him, or so he believed, forever.

However, around the bend in the river,
she popped back up to the surface,
and kept floating, floating, floating -
down that long, long river...


... this is her story.

I was tryin, really tryin,

Keep my head above the waves,

With a mouth so full of water,

Floated down to ol L.A.

There I caught a branch and pulled it,

Climbed upon the sturdy ground,

Looked about for dear ol father,

But ol dad was not around.

What a pickle! What a pity,
When I tripped into the brine,
Now my stomach's really growlin,
Wanting pancakes – maybe nine!

Needed kitchen, needed bowl,

Needed spoon to mix the eggs,

Come to think of it I needed,

More than eggs to fix this mess!

So I built a house of pancakes,

When I sold my mother's ring,

It was loved by all who came here,

Made more money than a king!

Every morning, eating pancakes,

Thought about ol poor ol pop,

I should travel, I should find you,

Now that I own thirty shops!

So I traveled up the coastline,

San Francisco and beyond,

Tried to locate my old father,

Every river, every pond.

Then I found him, tapped his shoulder,

Watched him jump into a tree,

Thought he surely saw a ghost there,

Lookin just like sweet ol me!

"Father! Father! It's your daughter,

It's your daughter, Clemy Tine."


"But I lost you in the water!

Thought I lost you, Clemy Tine!"

"I survived, dad,

I survived and,

I've been living in L.A.,

I've a mansion and a butler,

And a footman and a maid!"

In that cavern, in that canyon,

So he left his frying pan,

Hadn't mined but rocks and tadpoles,

And a toad and a tin can.

So they traveled,
And they traveled,
And they settled in L.A.,

"Have some pancakes, my dear daddy,
I won't leave you, not again……"

# THE END

# Oh My Darling, Clementine

In a cavern, in a canyon,
Excavating for a mine,
lived a miner forty niner,
And his daughter Clementine.

Oh my darling, oh my darling,
Oh my darling, Clementine!
You are lost and gone forever,
Dreadful sorry, Clementine.

Light she was and like a fairy,
And her shoes were number nine,
Wearing boxes, without topses,
Sandals were for Clementine.

Oh my darling, oh my darling,
Oh my darling, Clementine!
You are lost and gone forever,
Dreadful sorry, Clementine.

Drove the ducklings to the water,
Ev'ry morning just at nine,
Hit her foot against a splinter,
Fell into the foaming brine.

Oh my darling, oh my darling,
Oh my darling, Clementine!
You are lost and gone forever,
Dreadful sorry, Clementine.

Ruby lips above the water,
Blowing bubbles, soft and fine,
But, alas, I was no swimmer,
So I lost my Clementine.

Oh my darling, oh my darling,
Oh my darling, Clementine!
You are lost and gone forever,
Dreadful sorry, Clementine.